FIREWALL

LESSONS FROM LOCKDOWN

PAUL CANON HARRIS

KEVIN MAYHEW LTD

First published in 2020 by Kevin Mayhew Ltd,
Rattlesden,
Stowmarket,
Suffolk, IP14 3BW
www.kevinmayhew.com

ISBN (paperback) 978-1-8385-8090-2
ISBN (eBook) 978-1-8385-8091-9
Paperback product code 1501670
eBook product code 1501671

Created with Vellum

Dedicated to my wife Catherine,
my faithful companion in lockdown as in all of life.
I know I am a "lucky, lucky boy".

CONTENTS

INTRODUCTION

F*IREWALL* emerged from the experience of Spring 2020 when people across the world found their lives turned upside down by the Coronavirus. Tragically many lives were lost and yet there were positives that emerged as well. I remember thinking that there had probably never been a season of Lent in which so much was given up by so many. For years people had spoken about an accelerating lifestyle. Social media and the self-help publishing sector had spawned programmes and products designed to help people de-clutter, de-stress and chill out. Suddenly the prohibition on travel and on meeting families and friends, forced people to reappraise the way they did ordinary life. Everyone had to adjust. Schooling, church, shopping and leisure all had to be done differently. The internet came into its own as a force for good. Computer manufacturers and users had used the term "virus" as a technical term and now a medical version was the real present danger. In some of my other leadership and spirituality writing I had reflected on the dangers that modern life posed to our mental and spiritual well-being.

It was in this context that my publisher Dave Gatward and I had a conversation about producing an anthology resource focussed on keeping the stresses of life at bay. Life throws up a wide range of pressures that can wear us down and eventually overwhelm us. Pressure, whether external or internal, is a threat to our well-being. We can respond to pressures in different ways. Sometimes it is right to stand our ground, confront the cause and fight. Other times the right thing is to beat a hasty retreat. The epistles include advice to stand and resist the evil one (James 4:7) but to flee temptation (2 Tim.2:22). It is important in life to know whether you are running from or running to somewhere, to know when to stand firm and when to flee.

In *FIREWALL* you will find interactive bible studies, reflections and poetry that I hope will enable you to combat some of the threats to your own well-being. In many ways they are challenges that successive generations have had to face. I hope that you find these timeless lessons and contemporary reflections helpful.

March 2020 Bournemouth

HOW TO USE FIREWALL

IT'S EASY!

FIREWALL has been written to be used by individuals or as a group resource. You can read it sequentially or dip in at any point. If you read it all in one go – beware of indigestion. There are regular challenges and reflective questions. Try and allow time for these. A group session could include a study on the fuller Bible passage in each of the Self-Defence lessons and end with a reflection based on one of the poems.

I have included only a very short extract in each Bible reflection. You may want to read the passage in its fuller context.

SELF-DEFENCE MOVE #1

KNOW YOUR ENEMY

Numbers 13:17-19 – Moses sent out spies
When Moses sent them (spies) to explore Canaan, he said, "Go up through the Negev and on into the hill country. See what the land is like and whether the people there are strong or strong or weak, few or many. What kind of land do they live in? Is it good or bad? What kind of towns do they live in? Are they unwalled or fortified?

It is a matter of military orthodoxy that in warfare it is important to know as much as possible about your enemy. I am a fan of spy stories, real and imagined. They are proof positive of the length states will go to get to know their enemy. Health professionals when faced with a pandemic rely on the work of scientists to help them understand the nature of what they are confronting.

When it comes to protecting our mental, emotional and

spiritual wellbeing the same principle applies. We need to know what we are up against, not least because the battleground is often internal. In the area of work and ministry great emphasis is often put on knowing and playing to our strengths. This is undeniably important and yet in our context here it is equally important to examine our actual and potential weaknesses.

Parallels with a health context are instructive. Doctors try to identify symptoms in their patients. They know what to look out for; temperature, blood pressure, presence of a cough or a rash are all common physical indicators. Similarly, when assessing our own spiritual, emotional and mental health there is a well-known list to look out for. Sometimes our friends and relatives are also well-placed to comment. Some of the most common signs that all is not well are fear, envy, rage, guilt, weariness, repeated temptation, doubt and cynicism. Medical clinicians also test for under-lying health issues. Previous medical "adventures" – a phrase my then GP famously used – have left me with only one kidney and a slight issue with my heart. Most of the time I feel fine and like to think I look reasonably fit for my age. However, recent events forcefully reminded me that I need to take extra care not to be exposed to harm. Most people know what is meant by carrying baggage – unhelpful emotions that can come to the surface and interfere with everyday life. Most of us carry difficult memories - scar tissue from the past that can trip us up. Things to look out for are lingering hurts, the harbouring of on-going resentments or grievances and jealousy. When I travel, I know I must check my baggage allowance, if I am over my limit it may cost me dear. Stopping and taking stock of the baggage from the past is a good way of protecting myself from further damage. I have always loved Jesus' invitation "Come to me, all you that are weary and are carrying heavy burdens, and I will give you rest." (Matthew 11:28).

There is no inoculation against these negative factors and experiences. Being a Christian does not buy me an exemption clause from the knocks of life. However, Jesus does offer his help, forgiveness and healing in all its forms. With good reason is he sometimes referred to as the Great Physician.

Self-Check

What are your greatest challenges in life? Are there factors that hamper you in dealing with them?

Silence

Silence comes in aural shades:
golden, guilty, awkward.
Mute inner panic
a world away from peaceful stillness.

Silence is precursor of sound,
aftermath of noise.
Paradox and perfection,
it needs to be heard, listened for, received.

Silence is pregnant pause,
expectancy and promise.
Anthem of death,
dying echo's end.

Noiseless the chaotic void,
the eternal moment preceding
the Divine applause, the cymbal crash of the
hands of God,
the Big Bang of creation.

Modern life has a constant soundtrack, and notwithstanding personalized playlists in our earphones, it is often not of our choosing. Music, news and information is streamed our way, on tap 24/7. Many of us have never discovered the value and discipline of being silent. Often it is not possible until we have slowed down. It takes time to adjust to silence, because of the noise in our heads, different projects and people clamouring for our attention. I live by the sea. When I was young, I used to run into the water and dive headlong. These days if I did that, I would risk a coronary, so I make my way in more slowly. I give myself time to adjust to the temperature and the swell. Then I enjoy the refreshing coolness, the sense of buoyancy. Silence is like that. When I go on a silent retreat it takes a while to adjust – but it's lovely once you're in! A week or month away is impractical for most of us but – setting time aside regularly in a normal week is do-able and brings rich rewards.

Challenge

Settle down somewhere comfortable and spend fifteen minutes in complete silence. If it is a good experience – try it again for longer next time. If it is a struggle – have another go but try five minutes less. Persevere.

SELF-DEFENCE MOVE #2

MIND YOUR MIND

Romans 12:1-2 – Transformed not Conformed Therefore, I urge you, brothers and sisters, in view of God's mercy, to offer your bodies as a living sacrifice, holy and pleasing to God—this is your true and proper worship. Do not conform to the pattern of this world, but be transformed by the renewing of your mind. Then you will be able to test and approve what God's will is—his good, pleasing and perfect will.

Christians often use the word "heart" when describing how they sense God prompting and interacting with them. They don't mean the four-chambered blood pump in the human chest. They are trying to capture something of God being central to their life and being. This tendency has sometimes given the impression that the life of faith is all about touchy-feeling emotions with a diminished role for reason and the mind. In fact, Old and New Testament writers were clear that people's minds played a major part in the life of an authentic believer.

Following Jesus Christ was a conscious decision from the outset, and a lifetime of following him was a sequence of deliberate choices. The apostle Paul was a great thinker. He understood the pressures on people to conform to the ways of the world. He urged fellow Christians in Rome to "be transformed by the renewing" of their mind. (Romans 12:2). That challenge holds good today. This is not about mental agility but rather about being discerning and developing good patterns of thought.

The danger for the Christians in 1st century Rome then, and for us now is that we will be compromised by the dominant culture in which we find ourselves and lose our distinctiveness.

I am of an age at which the pop-up ads on my social media accounts urge me to do endless mind puzzles that will help me stave off senility. The Bible encourages us to re-calibrate our minds to stave off negative influences: "whatever is lovely, whatever is admirable, if anything is excellent or praiseworthy – think about such things." (Philippians 4:8)

Self-Check

On a scale of 1-10 how prone are you to being influenced by unhelpful pressures in society or in your more immediate situation?

This River

Stronger souls than you have tried
Youths with dreams and hopes and fears
No-one arrives unscathed on the other side

Pick your moment, choose your tide
Don't waste days and lose the years
Stronger souls than you have tried

Ask for help and swallow pride
Wisdom whispers into open ears
No-one arrives unscathed on the other side

Take what you need, put wealth aside
Fortunes fade as the ending nears
Stronger souls than you have tried

Tell others you will not be denied
Ignore the jibes, the jokes, the jeers
No-one arrives unscathed on the other side

Do not look back, win the fight inside
This river is broader than it first appears
Stronger souls than you have tried
No-one arrives unscathed on the other side

People who read this poem or hear it performed often jump to the conclusion that it is about preparing for impending death. Not a very cheery thought but a necessary exercise at some point in life. I understand why my readers make that assumption. My start point in writing in fact was reflecting on the journey from youth into adulthood and the mistakes most of us make along the way. I pictured an island of young people who could see another shore – the land called Adulthood. They had to choose when to strike out across a turbulent stretch of water. In real life this is rarely a smooth passage for any of us. Identifying those things and values that truly matter are crucial to arriving more-or-less in one piece. Of course, some other lessons are only learned after arrival. Equipping our young people for the journey is an important challenge and high calling.

Challenge

Make some space for yourself and look back on the seasons in life in which you learned important lessons. Then give time to consider any adjustments God may want you to make now.

SELF-DEFENCE MOVE #3

THE ARMOUR OF GOD

Ephesians 6:10-11,13 – A lesson from Lockdown Finally, be strong in the Lord and in His mighty power. Put on the full armour of God so that you can take your stand against the devil's schemes. ..Therefore put on the full armour of God, so that when the day of evil comes, you may be able to stand your ground, and after you have done everything to stand.

Paul the apostle had plenty of opportunity to study a Roman soldier's armour at close quarters. He was arrested at least three times and spent roughly five and a half years in custody – some of which seems to have been a form of house arrest. In Ephesians 6 he details each piece of protection his captors wore, using each piece as a metaphor for some aspect of God's protection of His people.

Over the years many Sunday School teachers and

preachers have dressed up children in different forms of military or sporting protective clothing – often to great comedic effect. It is reminiscent of when King Saul dressed up young David in his full-size armour to go and fight Goliath. David swiftly turned down the offer. (1 Samuel 17:38-40). David and Paul – both recognised that there was a spiritual element to the battles that they faced. Young David declared "All those gathered here will know that it is not by sword or spear that the Lord saves for the battle is the Lord's." (1 Samuel 17:47). Paul's key message to his readers was that they should use all of God's protection in their spiritual battle. There was no room for complacency.

We each have our own Achilles Heel. Contrary to much modern thinking it can be a sign of strength to know and admit our weaknesses. Denial or self-delusion are dangerous and a recipe for disaster. Knowledge and recognition of where and how we might be vulnerable is a useful first step only if we then go on to address them.

Often our greatest strength in extreme becomes a weakness e.g. the perfectionist who becomes a workaholic.

Self-Check

Is there any area of your life or personality trait that makes you vulnerable? Ask God to protect you specifically in this.

The Sea Is His

These waves are incapable of self-isolation, it
is beyond them.
No breaker ever struggled with loneliness or
singleness,
no ripple played gooseberry, no eddy joined
Tinder.
They are rebellious, unstoppable in their
defiance,
predictable, incessant and steady.
Accustomed to unsettling undercurrents,
shifting sands and varying tides,
they adjust and adapt to prevailing
conditions, to the sea state
be it slight, moderate or rough.
With metronomic rhythm they signal
dependability and order.
They never rest, take time off, feign sickness or
pull a snow day.
They will be here tomorrow, next week, next
month, next year,
whenever we surface, gasping for air, from
this season of fear.

I live by the sea and walk along the cliff tops or on the beach most days with my dog called Hope. At night when the town is still, I can hear the waves breaking on the beach. Their constant presence reassures me, especially when challenged by change in my personal life or on a national and even global level. The title of this poem, *The Sea is His,* is taken from Psalm 95 verse 5 "the sea is his and he made it". The psalmist turns quickly inland as he affirms his belief and trust in God's care, "for He is our God and we are the people of his pasture, the flock under his care." (Ps.95:7) It is important in turbulent times, when things seem out of control and overwhelming, to hold on to the sense that belief in God is a refuge. He will bring good out of bad times while comforting us now in our pain and confusion.

Challenge

Go for a walk and look for one thing in the natural world that speaks to you of God.

SELF-DEFENCE MOVE #4

BACKING OFF IS SOMETIMES BEST

Trouble in the Family - Jacob – Genesis 27: 43-44 When Rebekah was told what her older son Esau had said, she sent for her younger son Jacob and said to him, "Your brother Esau is consoling himself with the thought of killing you. Now then, my son, do what I say: Flee at once to my brother Laban in Haran. Stay there until your brother's fury subsides."

The family is meant to be a place of security and nourishment. Sadly, all too often family homes or the network of family relationships become battlegrounds. My wife Cathy and I raised four sons who now appear to be responsible adults. This still surprises us. Looking back, the air in our house seemed thick with testosterone. They were very competitive, there were frequent accusations of cheating in board games. "Boys stop fighting –

go in separate rooms till you have calmed down" was our regular response.

Jacob and Esau were non-identical twins, born late in life to older parents. It is fair to say that the upbringing they received from Isaac and Rebekah fostered jealousy rather than closeness. Esau was an outdoors type of guy. Jacob might be described as something of a "mummy's boy". Sibling rivalry came to a head when Jacob cheated Esau out of his birth-right and father's blessing. Watching your children fight is never a good experience. Rebekah urged her younger son to make his escape.

A strategic retreat gives space to calm down and allows others to get out of range. Jacob spent much of his early life on the run – from family, from enemies, even from God – largely, because of fear and guilt. Maturity brought stability and peace as he eventually fell in step with God's plan for his life.

Self-Check

If you have a relationship affected by jealousy, can you address it, or should you retreat?

Dystopian Spring

I walk deserted streets,
they lie where they have fallen
on pavements, in gutters, strewn across the
road.

Only days ago, I admired them, their freshness
and vigour,
enviable vitality, colours and figure.
How passing their beauty, their moment of
glory,
blown away by chill breeze
magnolia blooms trodden underfoot
tell a salutary story.

Tension between the generations is as old as the hills. The historical books in the Old Testament chronicle plenty of inter-generational strife. I remember my wife and I being struck by an insight we were given on a parenting course many years ago; "we find it exasperating when we see our own least attractive traits displayed in our children". Sometimes we experience a degree of nostalgia tinged with jealousy when we see their youthful vigour and belief that they are immortal. I wrote Dystopian Spring with mixed feelings. In part, I was frustrated by youngsters having a cavalier attitude to measures that would benefit everyone. I also frequently experience a desire to implore young people to make the most of the opportunities of youth while they have them.

Challenge

Start a conversation with or drop a note or email to a younger person and ask them what their dreams are?

SELF-DEFENCE MOVE #5

FLEE TEMPTATION

Joseph – Genesis 39:6b-7: 11-12 Joseph was well-built and handsome and after a while his master's wife took notice of him ... One day Joseph went into the house to attend to his duties, and none of the household servants was inside. She caught him by the cloak and said, "Come to bed with me!" But he left his cloak in her hand and ran out of the house."

Joseph appears to be an example of someone who knew the importance of fleeing temptation. I say "appears", because the Bible gives no description of Potiphar's wife and the historical assumption is that being a man he must have been tempted when his older mistress of the house propositioned him. The more pertinent issue is that he was expected to be her "obedient servant". He knew instinctively that it would be wrong on three accounts.

He would be wronging his master, His God and compromising his own values. Situations like this occur in modern life as they have done through the ages. Any of us may find ourselves in a situation that we know is fraught with moral danger. This dynamic applies as much to gossip or greed as it does to sexual temptation. Being tempted in and of itself is not a sin. The problems start when we give in. It is all too easy to blame others, circumstances and even God himself instead of taking responsibility ourselves.

As a young man I was given advice about the power of sexual attraction. A student worker warned me, "If you don't want to finish up in Boston, don't get on the Boston train." By all accounts 1st century Corinth was a city full of immorality and temptation. The Apostle Paul reassured the Christians there that God would not let them be tempted beyond their strength but would provide a way of escape. (1 Corinthians 10:13). There is usually a point when we can choose to escape. It's down to us to take it. Sometimes my first prayer has been, "God help me to want to look for the way of escape."

Purity and holiness are not primarily things God demands *from* us so much as things he wants *for* us.

Self-Check

Are there recurring temptations in your life? If so, what strategies do you have in place to combat them?

Social Distancing, March 2020

He sat on his normal bench nursing a tinny or
was the ale nursing him?
I had not seen him for months, had wondered
if he was one of this winter's causalities,
taken like a frail robin by frost and storm. We
greeted each other. I expressed relief.
He grinned back. I had missed his missing
teeth. We obediently observed the two
metres prescribed divide - I hoped it
didn't look like walking by on the other
side.
We chatted about locals we knew, most on the
brew, speculated on when
the frogspawn would appear in the pond,
spoke of spring and beyond.
Walking on I reflected on the nature of true
social distancing.
We are distanced by birth location, education,
economic opportunity, impecunity,
genetic predisposition, social dislocation,
personal choices and the so-called
cruel hand of fate. But we are united by our
common humanity and love of frogs.
It was good to have seen him, to welcome him
back to his perch with other returning
seasonal migrants.

Nearly all my working life has been with people, many of whom have found themselves down and out, on the margins of society. I have worked briefly as a police officer, as a youth worker and for a long time as a priest. Homelessness and social injustice are issues I return to regularly in my writing. This poem reflects my continuing determination not to be like one of the characters in Jesus' Good Samaritan parable who passes by on the other side, ignoring the need of the man who had been robbed. I often fail in this, but I want to resist hard-heartedness and mean-spiritedness as much as I can. Life has taught me that none of us are immune from falling on hard times. Writing this poem reminded me of the importance of looking for the common humanity and shared interest in everyone I meet, especially those from whom I might shy away.

Challenge

Go out of your way to smile at and greet someone you might normally be tempted to avoid.

SELF-DEFENCE MOVE #6

GUILTY SECRETS LEAVE US VULNERABLE

Moses – Exodus 2:11b-12,15 – Blood on his hands Moses saw an Egyptian beating a Hebrew, one of his own people. Glancing this way and that and seeing no-one, he killed the Egyptian and hid him in the sand. When Pharaoh heard of this, he tried to kill Moses. Moses fled from Pharaoh and went to live in Midian.

This dramatic episode was from Moses' youth. Having murder on your CV might not be the best thing for a future spiritual leader. That tells us much about the range of people God uses to serve him. Moses was at that stage in the growing-up process when discovering his roots was particularly important. Brought up in the royal palace, as though a Prince of Egypt, people knew that he was from the enslaved people Jewish people. Intervening impulsively, he killed an Egyptian and tried to cover up his crime. This led to him being caught out in hypocrisy. He thought he had got away with it. Like many he fled to pastures new – another person in a foreign land, a displaced person with a guilty secret. I know from experience that many ex-pat communities have people who are trying to put the past behind them and reinventing themselves. Most of us have things we think we've got away with, the things we think no-one else sees - our secret sins. Changing our geographical location does not automatically alter our internal guilty landscape. Facing up to what we have done and seeking God's forgiveness releases us from the fear of discovery and the burden of guilt.

Self-Check

Are you carrying a secret from your past? If so, ask God specifically to release you from the burden of carrying it. (That may or may NOT involve sharing it with someone else.)

Surrender

Surrender you asked for but not by demand,
surrender you offered as a gift,
but quitting a battle was not what I'd been
taught,
hoisting a white flag not in my thoughts.
That's when you whispered, sowed a word in
my ear,

Child so frightened of failing, being
overwhelmed,
you need to give in if you want to go on,
you need to give in if you want to go on,
it's not weakness or cowardice
but wild, wild bravery,
wild, wild bravery inspired by my son.

In times of national emergency, politicians are inclined to express their determination to combat whatever the problem may be in Churchillian terms, The famous wartime leader's phrase "We shall never surrender" is inspiring and admirable. Defeatism never achieves anything. However, there is a sense and a context in which the ability to surrender is a good thing. This poem, which a friend subsequently turned into a song, came to me almost as the finished article when I was in church one morning. I cannot pretend that is a regular occurrence – life would be simpler if it were. Sometimes I have struggled stubbornly to resolve a situation rather than looking to God give me wisdom and to bring peace in place of turmoil. Such bouts of wrestling may be with outside factors and influences. Often the battle has raged within me. The adage, "Let go and let God" still holds good.

Challenge

Set aside a time and reflect on any aspect of your life in which God may be wanting you to surrender.

SELF-DEFENCE MOVE #7

TIREDNESS TAKES ITS TOLL. RECOVERY TAKES TIME

Elijah – 1 Kings 19:3-4 – Fear and burn-out
Elijah was afraid and ran for his life. When he came to Beersheba in Judah, he left his servant there, while he himself went a day's journey into the desert. He came to a broom tree, sat down under it and prayed that he might die. "I have had enough, Lord," he said. "Take my life; I am no better than my ancestors."

Never being able to resist a pun I think of this as the Prophet at a Loss incident. Elijah was one of several God's servants who had to flee from an angry king. Life is a roller-coaster even for the great men and women of God. Hard on the heels of having seen God display his awesome power to the pagan prophets, Elijah came back to earth with a bump, running scared. He was burned out physically, emotionally and spiritually. He displayed the classic symptoms of depression. His perspective was skewed, he didn't want company or help and wished God would end his life. Eventually he lay down under a tree and fell asleep. Over the next few days God refreshed and restored him – meeting his physical need for sleep and food (the original Angel Cake?) before recommissioning him. If you read on in the chapter, you discover more about how God restored Elijah over a period. Contemporary leaders and writers might well be tempted to write a book or schedule a preaching tour to tell the story of the miraculous provision of food. That was only the beginning. Elijah needed sleep, nourishment and space before he could receive emotional and spiritual renewal. Over-busy people often keep running, partly out of habit and partly from fear of losing significance or position.

God dealt with Elijah tenderly in his burn-out, speaking to him in a whisper. Twice God asked him "What are you doing here?" It is a good question to ask ourselves on a regular basis.

Self-Check

What would you like to hear God gently whisper to you?

If I Don't . . .

If I don't unwind
I'll unravel.
If I don't slow up
I'll grind to a halt.
If I don't chill out

I'll burn out.
If I don't loosen my grip on things,
things will tighten their grip on me.
If I don't spend more time with my loved ones
My loved ones will have no more time
with me.
If I don't stop to draw breath,
I'll stop breathing.
If I don't stop to smell the roses
I'll be pushing up daisies.

I have never been much of a one for making resolutions along the lines of giving up chocolate or eating fewer chips. However, I am a great believer in stopping and taking stock of the different parts of my life, my work, my friendships and my family. I wrote "If I don't" one New Year's Eve. Medical challenges had forced me to adopt a more flexible lifestyle and a slower pace in life. This was largely a case of adjusting to reduced energy levels but like many people my diary can very quickly fill up and I find other people's agendas setting my pace. 2020 will long be remembered as a time when, due to exceptional circumstances, people were forced to cancel their schedules, change their patterns of working and slow up. It wasn't by any means easy to do and yet as people adjusted, they appreciated aspects of the enforced change of pace. Hobbies were rediscovered, postponed household projects completed, jigsaws dusted off and a daily walk enjoyed by many. People wondered if positive aspects of the new life could become the new normal going forward.

My poem was hinting at God's Sabbath principle of rest, learning afresh that there are rhythms of life throughout creation, seasons of renewal and regeneration are essential.

Challenge

Take some time to sit alone with your diary, calendar or schedule. Imagine you and God looking over it together. Is there anything that you need to stop or any new thing you want to start?

Lost Property

All his life he had left an amnesic trail,
belongings secreted in his wake
like a forgetful snail.

Keys, phones, pens all lost,
even wallets forgotten
at considerable cost.

His spoor, the debris of a busy life,
misplaced to the amusement of his children,
the frustration of his wife.

Things can be replaced online at leisure,
beliefs and friends are harder to find;
lose your baggage, guard your treasure.

"Hey Vicar! How much did he leave?" asked a local journalist after the funeral of a wealthy businessman. "All of it!" replied the vicar, or so the story goes. Most of us like to think we are not materialistic, but possessions are necessary and important. The key thing is to have them in the right place in our lives. There is a real danger that we prioritize things over people – sometimes without realising it. The person who always says "yes" to the extra shift, who regularly gets back after the kids have gone to bed – because he or she is providing for them may one day rue the saying "No-one ever had *I wish I'd spent more time at the office* on their gravestone." True contentment is hard to find and never found in things. The Apostle Paul described contentment as a secret to be learned (Philippians 4:12.) and wrote these words to his young friend and colleague Timothy: "Godliness with contentment is great gain." (1 Timothy 6:6).

Challenge

Make space to relax with a prized possession in front of you. Thank God for it and the reasons or memories it is important to you. Then spend a little time reflecting on your attitude to money and possessions generally.

SELF-DEFENCE MOVE #8

UNFINISHED BUSINESS WITH GOD LEAVES US VULNERABLE

Jonah – Jonah 1:2-3 – fleeing God's calling
The word of the Lord came to Jonah..." Go the great city of Nineveh and preach against it". But Jonah ran away from the Lord and headed for Tarshish. He went down to Joppa, where he found a ship bound for the port. After paying the fare, he went aboard and sailed for Tarshish to flee from the Lord.

Much of my life I have worked with and ministered to young people and students. I have seen many fine women and men at that stage determined to seek God's will for their life. I have never assumed that God's calling is only to be up front Christian ministers or workers. I know He wants people to be salt and light wherever they work. I also believe that having a sense of God's calling helps to keep us going when the going gets tough. Despite being a great advocate for people taking a “gap year”, I am sad to hear people in middle age look back wistfully and say their gap year was the high point of their life of radical obedience to God.

If Jonah was one of the Mister Men (in the famous children’s books and cartoons) it would be hard to decide whether he should be Mr Timid, Mr Naughty or Mr Angry. He was frightened and reluctant to obey God’s calling on his life. I can relate to that. Later, after his whale adventure, and having preached in Nineveh he became angry when God showed compassion on the city. What a mixed-up preacher!

God may call me to do something radical or to speak a message of his love to someone at any stage of life. Even now I may initially struggle to obey. The lesson of Jonah is that reluctant disciples can run but they can’t hide. Obedience sooner rather than later is better for all concerned. Failure to do so leaves us prone to lapse into tick-over mode, stuck on the side-lines and going through the motions.

Self-Check

Sit down with a piece of paper on which you can mark the year of your birth and the current year. Reflect on the time-line of your life – you could mark some of the highs and lows in your journey of faith with God. What might He be calling you to in this season of your life?

Wash Day

Feet washed
Cheek kissed
Tongue tied
Tears wept
Back whipped
Head crowned
Hands washed

Hung out to dry

Side pierced
Body wrapped

Stone rolled
Clothes folded

My sins……

As soon as a new virus emerges, whether medical or computer related – the race is on to find a cure or fix. On the basis that prevention is better than cure, the hunt for a vaccine is a priority for people working in public health and epidemiology. As I said at the outset, Christianity does not offer the equivalent of a vaccine when it comes to things such as temptation and suffering, those are part of being human. However, at the heart of the faith and over all human history the Cross of Jesus Christ towers as the ultimate symbol and means of healing, forgiveness and hope. In Wash Day I wanted to express the essential events and truth of the Passion of Jesus Christ as succinctly as possible. These momentous events are often dressed up in so many words – I wanted the truth to speak for itself.

Challenge

Take an unhurried bath (candles and soft music optional) or shower and reflect specifically on what sense you have of Jesus Christ making you clean. Is this something new or something you have known for a lifetime?

SELF-DEFENCE MOVE #9

UNADDRESSED DISAPPOINTMENT CAN LEAD TO CYNICISM

Peter – John 21:2-3. Fleeing disappointment Simon Peter, Thomas (called Didymus), Nathanael from Cana in Galilee, the sons of Zebedee, and two other disciples were together. "I'm going out to fish," Simon Peter told them, and they said, "We'll go with you."

I think that modern day Christians sometimes judge the recorded failings of the early disciples quite harshly. We forget that they were learning as they went along without the benefit of the New Testament as a written and inspired guide. In the immediate aftermath of Jesus' death, they had to process their grief, remember what Jesus had said and decide what to do all before being filled with God's Holy Spirit at Pentecost. The arrest, crucifixion and death of Jesus was a crushing disappointment to them.

There has been much debate through the years about

whether Peter was, in common parlance, "doing a runner" and calling it a day as a disciple. Returning to his roots and to what he knew, namely fishing, made sense and was not altogether unreasonable. Perhaps it was a classic response to grief. His dearest friend Jesus had died. Peter, himself was wracked with guilt due to his denial and was trying to make sense of Jesus' amazing resurrection appearances. He had to do something. Whatever was behind his decision to go fishing – he was carrying pain and emotional baggage. He did not realise it then but God, still intended him to play a key role in spreading the Good News of the Risen Christ. It would take a beach-side breakfast and a restorative "clear the air" walk with Jesus to get him right.

I am always unconvinced by Christians who say they have never been disappointed in their journey of faith. Either, they are in denial or have never expected much of God. I am part of a small group called Travelling Companions. We try to support and encourage each other in our faith. One of the ways we do this is by trying to be honest about disappointments such as prayers that, as yet, appear unanswered as well as our own failings. I have been disappointed by and with others in life, however, my greatest disappointments have been with myself for the times my life have been a denial of God's calling on my life. Peter's experience reminds me that Jesus comes after the runaways and draws them back into his loving purpose.

Self-Check

Are you carrying any sense of disappointment with God? Can you share it with a trusted friend and ask them to pray for you about it?

Beach Bubbles

I have thrown sticks into the sea for dogs,
skimmed stones on the sea for children,
scattered ashes on the sea for comfort,
and this morning watched bubbles on the
breeze,
catching the light, cavorting to the horizon
in joyous flight.
Simple yet profound
lifting my spirits
raising my sights.

Modern life often seems so complicated, there are so many demands competing for our attention. Future challenges loom large, career decisions, care of the elderly and financial provision for myself can rob me of joy in the present. Many people battle with stress and concern about mental health. It is hard to enjoy the simple pleasures in life. I live on the coast and love seeing the way beaches enable adults to regress healthily, to channel their inner child. Parents work away at the detail of an intricate sandcastle long after the children have moved on to another activity. On more than one occasion Jesus urged his followers and listeners to become more childlike in their approach to life. "I tell you the truth, unless you change and become like little children, you will never enter the kingdom of heaven." (Matthew 18:3). Throw off adult world-weariness, cynicism and complication – rediscover childlike trust and joie de vivre.

This poem records how I watched an elderly lady with a big bucket of washing up liquid losing herself in this simple and charming activity. She was the only person on the beach until I arrived. Watching large bubbles head out over the sea towards the far horizon is delightfully relaxing.

Challenge

Buy or make a bubble kit for YOU to enjoy – accompanying kids optional.

SELF-DEFENCE MOVE #10

GOD'S ASSESSMENT OF YOU MATTERS MOST

King Belshazzar – Daniel 5: 1, 5, 26-28. King Belshazzar gave a great banquet for a thousand of his nobles and drank wine with them... Suddenly the fingers of a human hand appeared and wrote on the plaster of the wall. (Daniel was called to interpret the writing) "God has numbered the days of your reign and brought it to an end, you have been weighed in the scales and found wanting, your kingdom is divided."

In momentous times the phrase "the writing is on the wall" is often written and heard. It is used to express the sense that time is up for a company or for a politician. Most people are unaware that those words are from the Bible. Fewer still will know what it means. Daniel was one of God's prophets who had to "operate behind enemy lines" when God's people were in exile in Babylon. Belshazzar the king overstepped the mark and was confronted with God's verdict on his life, delivered by strange writing on the wall and interpreted by Daniel. God's verdict boiled down to this: "Your days are numbered, you have been weighed in the scales and found wanting".

When life is going according to our plans, if we are being successful and praised by others (*"I wish" I hear some of you say)* it is easy to get ahead of ourselves and to believe our own PR. Without realising it, we may be setting ourselves up for a fall. The apostle Paul put it like this: "Do not think of yourself more highly than you ought, but rather think of yourself with sober judgement, in accordance with the measure of faith God has given you." (Romans 12:3). Self-praise is no praise, and false modesty fools few. We all have strengths and weaknesses. God is more interested in our character than any certificates or CVs.

Self-Check

To what extent do you know your strengths and weaknesses? If God was writing you a reference what do you think He would write?

Whose Are You?

(*After Selwyn Hughes*)

You're looking for identity
Looking for a role
You're looking to find yourself

Looking to save your soul

You like to think you're no man's slave
You live life as you please
You look down on your brothers
Proud you're not like one of these

You surround yourself with trappings
Try to live a life of ease
You laugh by day and fret at night
You cry when no-one sees

You don't know really who you are
What you're really worth
You don't know what your purpose is
Why you're filling space on earth
Oh! You don't know really who you are
Until you discover whose you are!

Evidence from psychologists and counsellors is that many people suffer stress around issues of their personal identity and sense of security. There is pressure in the media, broadcast and social, to conform to certain images, fashion, body shape and lifestyle. People are made to feel inadequate if they don't match up to these celebrity fantasy lives. Some years ago, the Christian organization I worked for paid for the entire staff to go away to a residential centre to have our personality types and strengths analysed. It is fair to say not everyone was enamoured with the idea. Folded arms and scowls spoke volumes. Then the wise speaker and writer

Selwyn Hughes addressed us. He put the exercise in context and won us over with the line; "You don't know who you are until you know whose you are!" God does not want us to be like insecure children uncertain of whether we are loved, unclear as to our purpose and not knowing to whom we belong. Knowing our essential worth and purpose is rooted in our relationship with Christ, is liberating and reassuring.

Challenge

Sit quietly for ten minutes with some form of ID in front of you (Driving Licence, Passport, Birth Certificate etc), Use the time to reflect on your sense of identity. Thank God that He knows you and loves you simply for who you are.

SELF-DEFENCE MOVE #11

SEE THE BIGGER CONTEXT, HOLD ON TO HOPE

The Resurrection of Jesus – Luke 24:1-6a
On the first day of the week, very early in the morning, the women took the spices they had prepared and went to the tomb. They found the stone rolled away from the tomb, but when they entered, they did not find the body of the Lord Jesus. While they were wondering about this, suddenly two men in clothes that gleamed like lightning stood beside them. In their fright the women bowed down with their faces to the ground, but the men said to them, "Why do you look for the living among the dead? He is not here; he has risen!"

In difficult times people wonder how long things can go on as they are. People look for light at the end of the tunnel, hope for a better day. I have already referred to the centrality of Jesus' crucifixion to the Christian faith. His death paradoxically is understood as the victory over sin and death, opening the possibility of forgiveness and life. The Cross should always be considered in tandem with the Empty Tomb, they are inextricably linked. The resurrection of Jesus by God the Father is the proof positive of that victory. It is the touchstone of truth for Christians. Paul spelled it out in many places, notably when writing to the Christians in Corinth: "If Christ has not been raised, our preaching is useless and so is your faith.....but Christ has indeed been raised from the dead," (1 Corinthians 15:14 and 20).

The term "worst case scenario" is frequently used in the face of difficulty. Christians value human life as a gift, and yet they know that the worst thing that can happen is that they die. For them it is not the ultimate tragedy because they hold on to the hope of heaven. Jesus had comforted a close friend in her grief for her brother with these words: "I am the resurrection and the life. Whoever believes in me will live, even though he dies, and whoever lives and believes in me will never die." (John 11:25-26). This promise of life can help us see challenges and trouble in this world in a new light.

Self-Check

Jesus spoke those words to Martha. He followed them up by asking her directly "Do you believe this?" How would you have answered him and what difference does it make to your life?

Choose Your Attitude

This glass is neither half full nor half empty.
It is the glass in my hand today,
the one I can enjoy
or pour away.
I can sip and savour
or neck it,
down it in one.
Make it last or drink it fast,
I'm easy either way.
This is not ambivalence,
simply a taste of reality,
a dose of common sense.
Life is seldom wholly good
rarely totally grim,
no point choking on my beer
for fear of what may come my way.
This glass is sufficient,
the one in my hand today,
the one I can enjoy
or choose to pour away.

When plans go awry, and things go wrong it is worth remembering that there is normally a point at which we can choose how we will respond. The title of this poem "Choose your attitude" is taken from the family motto of some friends. They were a large, exuberant and exceptionally creative household. In the rough and tumble of life inevitably people made mistakes and things did not always go according to plan. Family members would regularly remind each other of their motto - it often made a difference. I have watched the youngsters of that family grow into adult life. Some of them have had to face unexpected medical and career challenges at a relatively young stage. They have demonstrated resilience and held on to faith in the storm. The habit of choosing their attitude, learned when young, has stood them in good stead.

Challenge

Pour yourself any drink of your choice. Take time as you drink it to reflect on how the principle of *Choosing your attitude* can apply to your current circumstances.

SELF-DEFENCE MOVE #12

PACE YOUR RETURN AND EXPECT TURBULENCE!

A Return to "normal" life directed and managed by God. Nehemiah 1:1-2,2, 17-18

I had not been sad in the presence of the king before, so he asked me, "Why does your face look so sad when you are not ill? This can be nothing but sadness of heart. (1-2) Then I said to them (those who would do the work), "You see the trouble we are in: Jerusalem lies in ruins, and its gates have been burned with fire. Come, let us rebuild the wall of Jerusalem, and we will no longer be in disgrace. I also told them about the gracious hand of my God upon me and what the king had said to me. They replied, "Let us start rebuilding." So, they began this good work. (17-18)

When I was writing in the middle of the 2020 Covid-19 lock-down I could not decide what was the best analogy from the Bible for the situation in which we found ourselves. I thought about God's people on their extended route-march to the Promised Land and their phased return centuries later to Israel from exile in Babylon, In the New Testament I thought about Jesus' followers in prison and particularly Paul under house-arrest in Rome. His request for visitors to bring personal items from elsewhere resonated with me.

Ultimately, I decided the return from exile, going back to scenarios, landscape, routines and relationships that had been missed, best fitted the situation that faced people in my own country and without exaggeration, across the world. The account of Nehemiah in the Old Testament gives some of the best insights into what it was like. It also throws up timeless lessons which can work for us today.

The return from exile in Babylon was different from how the exodus from Egypt had been. It happened in stages and the return to the new normal post Covid-19 will of necessity be the same.

Nehemiah was the human catalyst for this great endeavour. If we read on in the book, we discover different stages to his strategy:

- **He reconnoitred**, took time to assess what would be needed (ch.2).
- **He began rebuilding**, incorporating what was left in the ruins as far as he could. He was building the new normal and it had to be a team effort. (ch.3).

- **He resisted and repelled opposition** (ch.4). Life after lockdown will be fashioned against a backdrop of pent up emotions which will lead to differences of opinions. Strong emotions are bottled up during any type of captivity. The experience of Terry Waite and other hostages in the past show that adjusting to freedom is rarely plain sailing in terms of mental and emotional health. Expect some white-water turbulence in relationships at home, at school and at work.
- **He redressed inequality and the needs of the poor**. (ch.5) During captivity and times of national difficulty, the pain and the damage is disproportionately spread. Nehemiah addressed this in practical ways. In the 21st century, the elderly, the poor, the lower paid, the minorities and the charities that serve them have taken the greatest hit.
- **He facilitated spiritual renewal**. (ch.8) Having addressed the infrastructure issues, Nehemiah then helped his people return to and renew their spiritual roots. He directed Ezra to read and remind the people of their holy writings, the Book of Moses, (ch.8). God's word hit home, people were moved to tears and asked forgiveness for how they had drifted away from Him. Lockdown has been/was an enforced time of retreat and reflection. People who were locked into a culture and lifestyles in the fast lane have been forced/enabled to slow down. They have

been able to access streamed religious content and worship from the privacy of their homes, without loss of face or embarrassment.

- **He rejoiced.** Party time! "*Go and enjoy choice food and sweet drinks, and send some to those who have nothing prepared. This day is sacred to our Lord. Do not grieve, for the joy of the Lord is your strength.*" (Ch.8) Getting straightened out and back on track with God is always a cause for celebrations.

Emerging from lockdown and the threat and presence of disease is always wonderful. It is marked by joyful reunions with those from whom we were separated. Stories are told. Freedom and other simple pleasures that were previously taken for granted are appreciated afresh. However, there is also mourning and remembrance for those who have died. People will need comfort but also, ironically, space to grieve. Some businesses do not survive such crises. People are made redundant. The old normal is gone, by definition a thing of the past. It can feel like revisiting a childhood home, fond memories tinged with nostalgia and sadness at what has changed. One can feel disorientated and irrationally offended at not being consulted over changes that have occurred.

Practical Steps

For all:

Pace yourself: sport was completely shut down, there was much speculation about when summer seasons might begin, and remaining matches and leagues be completed. Athletes know the importance of warming up, not just on competition day but in the run-up as well. New temporary daily routines need to be changed gradually. People need to begin to focus mentally on their work and duties in advance.

For parents and children:

- reassure children who may experience similar apprehension to when they first started school, or to that which they normally feel at the beginning of the school year. Let children know this is normal. It is ok for youngsters to take a comforting soft toy with them. They have had lots of time (for better or worse) with parents – they will miss this.
- Things like bedtimes and the amount of screen time should not be adjusted back in one fell swoop – do it gradually.
- Play dates and sleep overs will be fun. It may be wise to limit the numbers of children involved at any one time. Ease children back into socializing gently via small groups.
- Some families, having experienced home-

schooling may want to continue with that form of education. There will certainly be more provision in terms of resources than existed previously.

For teenagers, students and young people:

- variants of most of the suggestions about younger people (see above) apply. Social butterflies and party animals will probably throw themselves in to celebrations. People who are quieter, more introvert may not want to be forced into bonhomie and revelry.
- Drinking habits, sexual behaviour and drug use apparently changed for many during lockdown. People should be encouraged and enabled to stick to any resolutions they made about their life going forward. This piece of wisdom resonated with me recently: "It's okay to grow out of some people, including earlier versions of yourself". (anon – Facebook meme) Lockdown presented a clean slate – regression is not inevitable. This section applies as much to older people.
- Having had time to reflect can lead to greater self-awareness. This in turn, may mean that it is wise to seek helpful counselling over issues such as identity, aspirations and vulnerabilities.
- Opportunities to explore new hobbies or interests can now be pursued in a real setting, perhaps leading to new friendships.
- Young people should be encouraged to talk to

teachers, lecturers and academic counsellors about any anxiety they have in relation to exams, placements and applications.

For employers and employees:

- many sectors of business and industry throughout the economy are already familiar with the importance of phased returns after a period of illness or other prolonged absence. After nationwide lockdown, isolation and social distancing this should probably be the default for most of the workforce. People should not be expected to go from 0-60 in five minutes, we are not machines.
- Home-working and video-conferencing became the new norm. Some of these working practices that were forced on people may now become the work-mode of choice. There are advantages for people's well-being, home-lives and for the environment. In some sectors this may make economic sense for businesses. However, it is also true, that in most walks of life there comes a point when you "have to put skin on it"! Humans are intended for relationship.
- Many thousands of people were placed on furlough to safe-guard their income and the viability of companies. Furlough also produced insecurity for some; "Why was I furloughed, but not them?" HR departments and managers will need to address these issues with individuals.

- By the same token, some people may want to revisit their work arrangement, moving to more a flexible or part-time work pattern.
- There will be some who realise it is work that makes them unwell or unhappy. The desire to explore new work will be natural – though not necessarily easy in a challenging economic climate.

Self-check

This section on preparing to return is deliberately longer. Take time to reflect on those parts that apply most to you in your roles in life. These questions may help:

- How has lockdown felt for you? Did it feel like, exile, a journey to the promised land (perhaps of retirement) or like house-arrest?
- What does a phased return look like for you?
- Are there habits or relationships that have fallen by the wayside that are best left?

First Bath — Prisoner's Return

He stood in the attic bathroom savouring
privacy,
cool slate tiles welcome after searing sand.
Old pipes complained as the bath began to
fill,

coughing up spouts that slapped on the
smooth enamel,
worn with decades of travellers' tales.
He wiped condensation from the mirror,
studied his reflection;
hair wild and matted, lean frame streaked
with dust,
black dirt ingrained around his eyes, on his
neck, in hollows of skin;
inked detail on a grey watercolour wash.
He stepped carefully over the side,
standing a moment, adjusting to the stinging
heat.
He watched a layer of grime dissolve,
marbling like an artist's brush in a jam-jar.
He lowered himself exhaling loudly.
Oh yes, so ready for this. Bliss!
He sat cupping his groin, catching breath
before sliding down, stretching, flexing.
His feet left prints below the brass taps.
He toyed with the plug chain with his toes.
Submerged, he soaped his face,
dirt leaching from his hair.
He felt entombed, peaceful,
enwombed in his own water-world,
incarceration now a lifetime away from this
sensuous luxury.
He took his time, reading the tide-mark as it
formed,
remembering, trying to forget.

"For I know the plans I have for you," declares the Lord, "plans to prosper you, and not to harm you, plans to give you a future and a hope." **Jeremiah 29:11**

PAUL CANON HARRIS

Paul is a writer and broadcaster. He spent a short time as a police officer before training as a teacher and youth worker. He was ordained in 1984. Over the next 27 years he served in a variety of churches. For five years he was the Mission and Evangelism Secretary for Evangelical Alliance. He travelled widely in the UK and abroad training and encouraging church leaders. He is a Canon Emeritus of Gloucester Cathedral.

He lives in Bournemouth with his wife Cathy and their dog Hope. He broadcasts regularly on BBC Radio 2 and other stations. He performs poetry at festivals and events throughout the UK and abroad. He and Cathy have four adult sons and ten grandchildren.

Looking for more exciting resources?

OTHER BOOKS BY PAUL

Overturning Tables

Subversive poems for Christian worship

Jump Leads and Bump Starts

A year of unusual conversations with God

Leading for a Change

Searching questions and practical suggestions for church leaders

Season the Preaching

Inspiration from the Common Lectionary

Young Person's Quick Guide to Leadership

Essential resources for schools, uniformed organisations and sports clubs

---

With Heather Torrens

Lift Off

Leadership skills for children aged 7-12